HANGING ON BY THE

THREADS

Rev. Ronald Covington Sr.

Pastor R. Covington Sr.

Autograph Page

Rev. Ronald Covington Sr.

Scripture quotations taken from the Comparative Study Bible. Copyright © 1999 by Zondervan.

Howard Publishing Press LLC
"We Publish the Gift that God has given you."
P.O. Box 53504 Indianapolis, IN 46253
Website: www.howardpublishingpress.com
Email: howardpublishing@sbcglobal.net

Book Cover design by: Minister Sherri Wilson

Hanging On By The Threads

Phone: 317-529-9562

ISBN: 978-0-9893641-3-3

Printed in the U.S.A.

ACKNOWLEDGEMENTS

I want to first thank God, my Lord and Savior Jesus Christ for allowing and giving me strength to pen this publication in the midst of many emotional days, weeks, months, and years. I want to thank my wife Kim for collaborating with me, and for her love, patience, support, prayers, and encouragement through the good times, as well as, the tough times. I believe we both can identify with the song, "*I Want Complain*," sung by the late Rev. Paul Jones. The journey has been rough at times, but through it all, God has given us what we need to sustain us. I love you, and thank you for being there. I also want to thank the Friendship Missionary Baptist Church, where God has allowed me to serve for nearly 18 years. Thank you for your encouragement and support across the years.

Pastor R. Covington Sr.

DEDICATION

This book is dedicated to my dear wife Kim, my four wonderful children, Ronald Jr., Rev. Rick, Rhea, and Cameron, and to my loving mother, Mrs. Aline Scott Covington, who has gone to be with the Lord, and who I cherish and miss so much. To my brothers, George, John (Punch), deceased, Gilbert (Tiny), Donald, and my sister Mable. Thank God for all that you have meant and still mean in my life.

This book is also dedicated to all those who have faced tragedy and are facing tragedy in your life at this moment. I pray that this book will be a source of help, strength, and encouragement for you, as you travel through the valley of circumstances. As you read this book, I encourage you to pray, meditate on the Word of God, and know this. The sun will shine after while!

Pastor R. Covington Sr.

Table Of Contents

Chapter One

When Life Takes A Sudden Turn

Growing up as a child, you really don't think much about life, until you start actually experiencing life. As a child, we don't have many worries, if any. We just live second by second, minute by minute, hour by hour and day by day. We laugh, we play, we cry, we sometimes fight and make up, but most of all we just have fun. We're able to do all of this, because of our dependency on somebody other than ourselves. Our Parents! For most of us, as children, the only thing we thought about life was just living it. However, most of the time we do it casually and sometimes carelessly. What we don't realize is, that while we are living it up, those seconds turn into minutes, those minutes turn into hours, those hours turn into days, those days turn into weeks, those weeks turn into months, and those months turn into years. Then all of the sudden we find ourselves seemingly living in a whole different world. The nest changes for our good. The props that used to hold us on every level are dwindling. The responsibilities that we thought never existed, have now surfaced. We see things entirely different than what we used to. We begin to realize that this thing called life is serious. We have a brand new appreciation for the "good old days." How many times have we found ourselves rewinding the tape recorders of our lives to see just how good we had it?

Yes, growing up brings about a change. Our thoughts are different, our dreams are different, and our perspective on life is different. We grow up. We find ourselves in the place that Paul talks about in 1 Corinthians 13:11, *"When I was a child, I spake as a child, I understood as a child, I thought as a child: but when I became a man, I put away childish things."* The idea is that when we mature, childish things, talks and thoughts fade away. We are now faced with struggles and challenges, we had no way of knowing they would be coming our way. Truthfully, we win some and we lose some. That's the reality that we're faced with in our childhood, adolescent, and adult life. As we grow and mature we don't view life the same. We know now that, not only is life serious, but life can take a sudden turn.

In chapter one of the Book of Job, there's a conversation going on between God and Satan. In this conversation, God questions Satan concerning his previous whereabouts. He says to him, "*Whence comest thou*?" Satan responds to God saying, "*From going to and fro in the earth, and from walking up and down in it*" (Job 1:7). Job does not specify what Satan was doing while going and walking, but we get a glimpse of his persona in 1 Peter 5:8. It says, "*Satan walks about seeking whom he may devour.*" Satan hasn't changed. He was busy then, and is busy now, seeking someone to devour. His purpose was to get Job to curse God, turn his back on God and deny God. Let us all be aware that Satan still has that same purpose in mind in the time that we are living. He will use any means possible to get us to deny God, to doubt God and to turn our backs on God. BY ANY MEANS! Any means then, and any means now. He is the master of deceit. In Job's time he used tragedy, sickness and even tried to use Job's wife to discourage him. AGAIN, BY ANY MEANS! Being aware of this, we must diligently be on guard for the wiles and tricks of our adversary the devil (Eph. 6:11). Job's lesson teaches us first that life is uncertain and full of changes. One day we can be up and the next day down. One minute the climate of our lives can change from partly sunny to partly cloudy.

Pastor R. Covington Sr.

When I was a child growing up, I use to hear a song that I didn't fully understand until I got older. The title of that song is, *"Everything Must Change."* Beloved, life is full of changes, and these changes affect all of us. As each of us travel through the cycles of life, we go through changes. We go from infancy to childhood, from childhood to adolescence, from adolescence to young adult, from young adult to adulthood, from adulthood to middle-aged, and from middle-aged to senior. The last change is a transition from time to eternity. The song says, *"Everything Must Change."* Seasons change, expectations change, love changes, and no matter how much unshakable faith you have in something or someone, along comes a big or little alteration that will change your mind. Again, the title says, *"Everything Must Change."* While that's true to a certain extent, it's good to know that in this changing time, we have a God that doesn't change. The immutability of God (that He doesn't change) is clearly taught in Scripture. He says to us in Malachi 3:6, *"I am the Lord, I change not..."* Beloved, your circumstances may change. Your condition may change. Your case may change, but we have the assurance of the God that doesn't change. He's the same yesterday, today and forever (Hebrews 13:8). That's Good News!

Secondly, Job's lesson teaches us that it doesn't matter who you are, what you have, or how **"good"** you are, none of us are exempt from the trials and tribulations of this life. Trouble is the common denominator for all human kind. The wealthy, the poor, the white, the black, the fat, the skinny, the saved, the unsaved, you and me, we all have trouble and turbulence in our lives. In fact, we find in Job 14:1 these words. *"Man, that is born of a woman, is of a few days, and full of trouble."* The fact is, because we all are born of a woman, our life is short and troublesome in contrast to Adam who was formed by God and lived nine hundred and thirty years. Psalms 34:19 states, *"Many are the afflictions of the righteous, but the Lord delivers him out of them all."* Yes the righteous, those who are God's children are not exempt. Nevertheless, the good news is, we can expect God's deliverance. These words, spoken thousands of years ago, express the sentiment of millions living today. We discover in Job that he was rich, blameless, upright, and a hater of evil, and yet his world collapsed all around him. In one day, Job went from splendor to poverty. He went from riches to rags. What he lost affected his finances, his frame and his family. He lost his animals, his children, his health, and even the support of his wife. I've always heard that if the devil can't get to you, he will get to someone you love, in order to get to you. This saying became a reality in my life during the summer of 2003.

After serving Friendship Missionary Baptist Church as pastor for eight years, the Lord was speaking to me concerning taking the church to another level. Everything was going great in my life. I was really excited about where the Lord was leading us as a church. Everyone in my family was healthy and doing as well as anyone else. Then out of nowhere, my son's life, my life, our entire family life took a sudden turn that would affect us unto eternity. Again, if Satan can't get to you, he will get to someone you love. In Genesis 2:16-17, scripture lets us know that God gave the prohibition mandate to Adam, even before Eve was made from his rib. He says to Adam, "*Of every tree in the garden thou mayest freely eat: but of the tree of knowledge of good and evil.*" He even warned Adam, that in the day you eat the fruit off of the forbidden tree, that he would surely die. The next thing He did was inform Adam of something that Adam didn't know, *"It was not good that the man should be alone; I will make him an help meet for him"* (Genesis 2:18). The prohibition was given to Adam, but notice who Satan came to first, not Adam, but Eve, in which he deceived Eve. Satan deceived Eve through a clever combination of outright lies, half-truths, and falsehoods disguised as truth. Satan still uses this combination today. Satan can dress a lie up until it looks good. He planted seeds of doubt in Eve's mind. Beloved, this is where Satan plays his games. Spiritual warfare takes place in the mind of every believer in Christ. We wrestle and struggle in our minds every day against the devil. The mind encompasses our thoughts imaginations, reasoning, intellect, emotions and will. Our mind controls what we do or don't do. That's why it's important for us to guard our minds. We have to purposely, *"let this mind be in you, which was also in Christ Jesus"* (Philippians 2:5). As children of God, we must take the mind of Christ and let it flow in us.

Satan deceived Eve by causing her to make her decision based on what she could see, and on what her emotions and reason told her to be right. Isn't that what we do at times? Instead of trusting God, we trust what we can see, or we move or don't move based on our emotions, Webster's Dictionary defines emotions as, "conscious mental reactions (as anger or fear) subjectively experienced as strong feelings usually directed towards a specific object." We all have them and if we are honest, they sometimes have us going forward and backward, depending on how we feel. Our emotions can change from day to day, and sometimes hour to hour, depending on the circumstance. Again, we all have them, but problems come when our emotions have us. Many things have happened, many lives and families have been changed, a lot of dreams have been shattered, simply because someone allowed their emotions to have and take control of them. The circumstances of our lives make us more aware of things that are happening around us and in us every day of our lives. I've always had emotions. I've seen others express their emotions, but now because of circumstances, I find myself paying more attention to my emotions. I'm not only more aware of my emotions, but also the reactions of my emotions, as well as, the reaction of others to their emotions. I had to learn and I believe all us have to learn, that we shouldn't let our emotions be our master. We are not suppose to allow anything to be our master, but God. Easy? No, but it's just like sin. If we don't take control over sin, sin will take control over us. Romans 6:14 states, *"for sin shall not have dominion over you: for ye are not under the law, but under grace."* Beloved, we were created to have control, to have dominion, over every one of our emotions, whatever they may be. God has given us, men and women, authority over our emotions. Also, we can forget about the notion that women have more emotions than men. No, we all have the same emotions, we just react differently to our emotions. Women normally have an outward expression of their emotions, while men because of our macho-ness, internalize our emotions. Is it a wonder that we die quicker?

Satan not only deceived Eve by causing her to make her decision based on her emotions, but he also distorted God's Word and lied to make Eve doubt God's Word. Please note this, Satan still uses these tactics today. He still finds ways to distort God's Word, sometimes to make them appear harsher than they are, and sometimes to water them down to change their meaning so we can justify what we do or don't do. Satan is clever. He uses any means that he can to get us off focus, hoping to persuade us to distrust and deny God. In Job's time, he used tragedy, sickness, and even tried to use Job's wife to discourage him. Same devil, same tricks, different people, different days.

Chapter Two
Smooth Sailing And Then!

Again, everybody in my family was healthy and doing as well as anyone else. Then out of nowhere, it was as if I was a passenger, traveling on the ship with Jesus and His disciples on their way to Gadara in Mark 4:36-41. This passage really brings us to a reality as it goes against the grain of this new "Prosperity," "Name It And Claim It," "You don't have any trouble, all you need is faith in God" "You'll Never Be Sick or Broke Anymore," and "Call Those Things Which Be Not As Though They Were" theology. This dangerous and damaging theology has permeated the pulpits across this nation, giving a false hope to believers who refuse to do as 2nd Timothy 2:15, instructs us to do. *"Study to shew thyself approved unto God, a workman that needeth not to be ashamed, rightly dividing the word of truth."* The truth is God's idea of prosperity has nothing to do with what we have. We can name and claim anything, but if it's not in the Sovereign will of God, we are not only, not in His will, but futility is present with us. Faith in God, doesn't exempt us from trouble. The Word of God never tells us that we will not be sick. It does tell us in Exodus 15:26, *"that God is the God that heals thee."* We cannot call those things, which be not as though they were. When we exegete the text correctly, we discover that it's talking about God, not us.

The text in Mark lets us know that Jesus had a long, frustrating and emotional day. First, He confronts the Scribes who are accusing Him of being in partnership with Satan. Secondly, He has to deal with His mother and His brothers coming to rescue Him and take Him back to Nazareth. Finally, at the time of our text, He is exhausted from teaching in parables by the seaside. In verse thirty-five Jesus instructs His disciples to cross over to the other side of the Sea of Galilee. He gives them the order to pull out, but He doesn't pull out on them. I've discovered that there are people who will send you to places that they are not willing to go themselves. They will ask you to do things that they don't dare to do themselves. Jesus says to them, *"Let us cross over."* In other words, Jesus is not just sending them, He's also going with them. The shouting point for every believer is that the Lord goes with us and is with us. In the Gospel of Matthew, the Lord commissions us with a promise. He says *"Go ye therefore, and teach all nations, baptizing them in the name of the Father, and of the Son, and of the Holy Ghost: Teaching them to observe all things whatsoever I have commanded you: and, lo, I am with you alway, even unto the end of the world. Amen"* (Matthew 28:19-20).

They take off and eventually a storm arises, but the good news is that Jesus was on board of the ship when the storm arose. The winds started blowing and the waves began to beat against the ship but it didn't affect Jesus. I'll say something about that in a minute. The reality is that you can have Jesus in your life and a storm can still come. In fact, storms will come whether you have Jesus in your life or not. Sometimes life has a way of throwing you a curve when you least expect it. Sometimes life will take a sudden turn. The good news is that with Jesus, you can experience rest and peace right in the midst of your storm. What He promises is not His protection from the storm, but His presence in the storm. The Psalmist David would tell you that God never promised that we would never be in the valley, but His presence would be with us. The disciples and Jesus are on their way to the other side. We discover in the text that when they first took off it was smooth sailing and suddenly a storm arose. That's the way it is in life. Some storms do come suddenly. You can be sailing through life with everything going well and all of the sudden a storm can arise and your bottom can drop out.

In one night, everything changed for me and my family for the rest of our lives. In one night, it seemed as if our whole world was collapsing around us. In one night, I went from being on cloud nine to ground zero. In one night and in the days to follow, I went from hanging on to the strong rope of hope and faith to hanging on by the threads. My life, our life, had suddenly taken a swift turn. Night turned to midnight. At this time for me, there was no light at the end of the tunnel. I have never liked roller coasters, but on this night, I found myself riding on the worst roller coaster of my life. I went from one emotion to another seemingly at the same time. Fear, love, hurt, sorrow, and finally failure. I began to ask those age-old questions, why us? What could I have done differently? My mind kept taking me to "If". If I had been there, things would have turned out a lot better. If only I had gotten a phone call, we wouldn't be living this nightmare. The reality was and still is, life is tough and it happens to all of us. No matter how much I wanted to push the rewind button, this tape was still going to play the same thing. All I could do was to find a place of solitude and cry, "Oh God Help Me!" I knew then that with all the education that I had, with all the family and friends that I had, with all the money that I had, I needed something, rather someone greater than all of these things to help me during that moment. This was the toughest and seemingly longest night that I had ever had. I found myself over and over again, wishing that this night was a dream and all I had to do was wake up. No dream, this was reality! Life for us had taken a sudden change. For me, weeping really endured for the night and the thought of joy coming in the morning was not even a passing thought. It was smooth sailing for us, "But Then."

Yes, it was smooth sailing for the disciples but then suddenly a storm arose. As I stated before, the winds and the waves didn't affect Jesus. It wasn't the storm that woke Jesus up, it was the cry of His disciples. The good news for us is that whenever we are caught up in our storm, the Lord will hear us when we cry. That's why I love that old church hymn, "*I love the Lord, he heard my cry."*

It's storming, the waves are beating against the boat, and the disciples panic. The good news is, the disciples knew where to go and who to turn to. When trouble comes, in the midst of storms, you've got to know where to go and who to turn to. Often times when trouble comes in our lives, we have a tendency to go to the wrong places and the wrong people who really can't help us. Jesus was in the hinder part of the ship asleep on a pillow. In Mark 4:35 it says, that a storm arose, but when you read verse 39 the text says, Jesus arose. Whenever a storm shows up in your life, we can rest assured that Jesus will also show up, and when He shows up, He always shows out. When Jesus disciples awoke Him, they asked Him a question that they should have already known the answer. They asked Him if He cared. What a question. After all, they had previously been called by and cared for by Jesus. They had witnessed His conduct and character for several years. They were there when Jesus healed Peter's mother-in-law. They were there when Jesus healed the man sick with the palsy that they let down through the roof. They were there when Jesus healed the man with the withered hand on the Sabbath. Now He is with them on a ship in a storm. Does He care? Yes, He does, and I want to encourage somebody today, and let you know that whatever you are going through, HE CARES! He really cares. In fact, the Apostle Paul lets us know in 1 Peter 5:7 that we can, *"Cast all your care upon him; for he careth for you."* Jesus gets up and speaks up. He rebukes the wind and says unto the sea, "Peace be still." The Bible says, *"the wind ceased"* and there was a great calm. Beloved, just as Jesus spoke to His disciple's situation, He can and will speak peace to our situations. He does this because HE CARES!

Pastor R. Covington Sr.

Chapter Three

Good People Doing Bad Things

Throughout the Word of God, there are examples of good people who did bad things. Abraham, the father of faith, lied concerning his wife. Moses, a deliverer killed an Egyptian. Noah, a builder got drunk. David, a man after God's own heart committed adultery and had Uriah killed, etc. This reality goes beyond the Biblical days and finds itself present in our day and time. The list includes presidents, preachers, sports figures, politicians, entertainers, etc. When we think about it, the list can really include all of us who call ourselves "good people." Actually, none of us can boast about being good. In the Gospels Jesus is responding to the "Rich Young Ruler" who addresses Him as "Good Master." Jesus tells him that there is none good but one, that is God. What Jesus was really saying to him was, "If you see that I am good, it is because I am God." Jesus was trying to sway the man's thinking toward accepting Him as Christ, the Son of God. Again, we all have to refrain from boasting because our goodness is not found in us, but in the Jesus Christ in us. The truth is, we have all done something bad, and we just were not caught.

Pastor R. Covington Sr.

All of us have bone and cartilage hidden in our closets. The only reason why we haven't become a statistic is because grace found us. Noah is not the only one that found grace in the eyes of the Lord. All of us can sing *"Amazing Grace how sweet the sound that saved a wretch like me."*

My oldest son, one of the most thoughtful, respectable, giving, and loving personalities that I know, had everything positive going for him in his life. He had a relationship with Jesus Christ, a great work ethic, along with a great job. He had a beautiful home where he was raising his children, when suddenly in a moment of anger, he committed a crime that eventually led to him facing the death penalty. There is a commonality that exists among all the personalities listed earlier in the chapter, and that's that they all claimed a relationship with God. The question is what would cause a good person with a relationship with God to do bad things?

First, we may not want to admit it, but it's within all of us, the capacity to do evil. There's within all of us, black, white, rich, poor, educated, and uneducated, the ability to do wrong. This ability and capacity is not predicated on where we live, what we have, or who we are. It doesn't matter who we know, or who knows us. It doesn't matter if we are churched or "unchurched", saved or unsaved. Our ethnicity and social status is not a prevention mechanism. All we have to do is be born. David, a man after God's own heart states in Psalms 51, *"Behold I was shapen in iniquity, and in sin did my mother conceive me."* The sin nature that we were born with makes us a sinner, not what we do. We are not a sinner because we sin. We sin because we are a sinner. Listen, if anybody had it going on and had bragging rights it was the Apostle Paul. Look at his resume. He was circumcised the eighth day, which meant that he was ceremonially clean. He was of the stock of Israel, which dealt with his special relationship with God. He was of the tribe of Benjamin, the elite tribe. He was a Hebrew of Hebrews, which meant he was a true descendant of David through Abraham. He wrote thirteen epistles in the New Testament. He went on three missionary journeys and planted churches. He was all of this, and did all of these things, and yet he says in the book of Romans, chapter seven, *"For I know that in me (that is, in my flesh,) dwelleth no good thing, and "O wretched man that I am! who shall deliver me from the body of this death?"* I know there are those who make themselves judges, who look at the faults of others and declare what they wouldn't do. Believe me, none of us knows what we will or will not do if the right circumstance confronts us. We know what we haven't done, but we don't know what we will do. All we can do is hope and pray that we will do the right thing at the right time, in all circumstances. Our daily song ought to be *"Search Me Lord."* We are to want the Lord to search us, because He knows all about us. He has perfect knowledge of us, and all our thoughts and actions are open before Him. David in Psalms 139:1-3, *"O Lord, you have searched me [thoroughly] and have known me. You know my downsitting and my uprising; You understand my thought afar off. You sift and search out my path and my lying down, and You are acquainted with all my ways."*

Secondly, we are involved in what is called spiritual warfare. When we became a Christian, we stepped right into the heat of an age-old battle. We have a three-fold enemy: the world, the devil, and the flesh. When the Bible speaks of the "world" in this context, it's referring to the sinful, rebellious world system. A system that changes. This is the world that loves the darkness and hates the light (John 3:20). In Romans 12:2, the Apostle Paul gives us a challenge. *"And be not conformed to this world (age): but be ye transformed by the renewing of your mind, that ye may prove what is that good, and acceptable, and perfect, will of God."* To conform is to copy the behavior and customs of the present world's system. It's to pattern ourselves after the changes of the world. It's the appearance of a person that changes from day to day, month to month, and year to year. I believe that if we would stop and take the time to look, we would see a gradual conformity of the church to the world's system. It did not happen all at once, but again the "deceiver" has been busy while we've been asleep.

We need to wake up and see that there's a battle going on in every individual, every family, and every church. The question is how do we win the battle? We simply win the battle over the world first, by not conforming to it. Conforming means to take on the form of something else. In Romans 12:2, is Paul speaking of the church or us as individual Christians? I believe he is speaking to both. Secondly, we win by becoming transformed. The Greek word for trans-formed is, "metamorphoo" where we get the word metamorphosis, which means to change. Conformity is outward behavior that comes from an outward source, while transformation is a change from within that leads to a change of outward behavior. We really have to be careful what we read and watch. Say what you will, but the media does have an effect on the thought process of our society. It did when I was growing up and it still does today. What we see glamorized today was glamorized when I was a youngster growing up in Haughville. The only difference now is that the media has become more graphic, sensual and violent. Years ago, when I watched Goldie in the movie "The Mack" I was impressed. The movie had such an impression on me, that when the movie was over, I wanted to be just like Goldie. I wanted the gold, the women, the fine car and the money. The interesting thing is, before I saw the movie, none of those things had overwhelmed my mind. The same thing goes on today with many of our youth. They see some of the same things glamorized, with a lot more glamori-zation. Back then, the gold was on a chain and on his fingers, but now the "players" wear the gold on their teeth. Back in the day, maybe you saw cleavage and thighs, but today, you see everything. If you are older than fifty, you remember Ozzie and Harriet or Ward and June Cleaver. When they went to bed, or rather beds, because they slept in separate beds, all you would see was pajamas. Those days are gone with the wind. You didn't see the oozies, and "Saturday Night" specials in the hands of young people killing each other. Society has glorified all of this violence, sex, and immorality to the point that it has affected the way many of our young people think. The X-Box games that our children play, the cartoons they watch, the music they listen to, are getting more sexual and violent. Our children aren't interested in Popeye and Janie, Bug's Bunny or the Flintstones. Reality shows have seized the spotlight on everyday television. The battle line for right or wrong, God's way or the world's way has been drawn. We may not want to admit it, but there is a battle for our souls going on. And if we are going to win this battle we must go through a radical change. I do know and I will be the first to admit that change doesn't come easy, but if we want to have victory we must be willing to change. We do this by the renewing of our mind by the spirit of God. With the aid of the Holy Spirit, we have to change our whole thought process.

The mind is a powerful force that dictates our behavior. The domain for the battle is our mind. The devil attacks us through our mind, which is why we have to guard our minds. Joyce Meyer wrote a tremendous book titled, *"The Battlefield Of The Mind."* We have to be careful what we feed our minds and what we allow to infiltrate our minds. Sometimes without even noticing it, we give the devil free access to invade our thoughts and we find ourselves thinking ungodly things. If we think about something long enough, we wind up doing that which we thought about. Our mind controls what our body does. Our bodies go where our minds go. Think about it, It's possible that if David had not continually thought about Bathsheba after seeing her in 2nd Samuel 11, he may not have sent for her, which eventually led to him committing adultery and murder. Your every move begins with a thought. The mind encompasses our thoughts imaginations, reasoning, intellect, emotions and will. Our minds control what we do or don't do. Again, that's why it's important for us to guard our minds. We have to purposely "*let this mind be in us which was also in Christ Jesus*" (Philippians 2:5). The key word is "let." God isn't going to force you to have the mind of Christ. Whatever you want to happen to your mind, you have to let it happen, whether good or bad. No one can control your mind unless you let them, not even Satan. Too many times, we give permission to Satan and others, as we allow them to infiltrate our minds and put their garbage in us. Be sure of this, whatever you fill your mind with that you will become. "*As a man thinketh, so is he*" (Proverbs 23:7). If a man keeps his mind and thoughts in the gutter, he becomes part of the filth in the gutter. We've all heard of "Stinkin Thinkin." If he keeps his mind upon the good, he becomes what we call good. If he focuses upon achievement and success, he achieves and succeeds. If his thoughts are focused upon God and righteousness, he becomes godly and righteous (not self-righteous). A man becomes and does what he thinks.

There's the carnal mind and a spiritual mind. The carnal mind is the mind of man's flesh or body. It's the mind with which man is born, the fleshly mind which he inherits from his parents. Have you ever noticed that you don't have to teach or tell an infant to think or act wrong? I have a six-year-old son, and one of the first words he started saying after mommy and daddy was, NO! The strange thing is that he said "No" with an attitude. A carnal mind is any mind that is not focused upon God, or the things of God. Listen, if our minds are not focused on God, then they will be focused on the devil and his things. We must as children of God, take the mind of Christ and let it flow in us. Whoever or whatever has our mind will control us. You've heard that old expression, give the devil an inch and he will take a mile. Beloved again, guard your mind from the snares of Satan. The questions for us are, how do we win this battle of the mind? How do we keep others from dumping and filling our minds with ungodly "stuff ?"

The spiritual mind is the natural mind of man that has been renewed by the Spirit of God. Unless we allow our minds to be renewed by the Spirit, we will continue to think and do the same things that we've always done. That's why it's of the utmost importance that we do as Ephesians 5:18 says, *"Be filled with the Spirit"* We need to declare war now! We need to take back that which Satan has taken, but again how?

Pastor R. Covington Sr.

We must totally immerse ourselves in the Word of God by daily meditating on what it says and not only that, but apply it to our lives. Once we totally fill our minds with the Word of God, there's no space left for the devil to come in and invade our minds. This is not a new idea. I didn't just receive this illumination. I remember as a child, the saints of old would sing *"I woke up this morning with my mind stayed on Jesus."* Somehow, they knew that their morning would be better if it started off with Jesus. However, they didn't stop there, they wanted to have a great day, so they continued the day with their mind stayed on Jesus. Again, guard your mind.

The second enemy is the devil. Regardless if some don't believe in the devil, he's real. Again, Peter warns the believer in 1 Peter 5:8, *"Be sober, be vigilant; because your adversary the devil, as a roaring lion, walketh about, seeking whom he may devour."* Why does the devil seek to devour us? His ultimate goal is not to just hurt us, but to hurt God. He wants to cut the heart of God. He wants to turn us away from trusting and obeying God. He wants us to doubt the presence, power and provision of God in our lives. He is the deceiver, the one who stands opposed to God and to all that God stands for. He is not our friend. In fact, Peter calls him our adversary. He is our enemy, our opponent, that we have to wrestle with each and every day. We can't let one guard down because Satan never lets down and watches for us to be off our guard. Jesus had a confrontation with him after spending forty days in the wilderness. He comes to Jesus and tempts him three times. Listen, if the devil tempted Jesus, be sure he will tempt any of us. He knows us and he knows our weakness. He knows just where to tempt us. He tempted Jesus in the wilderness, where a person really has a need. Jesus had fasted forty days and forty nights, afterwards He was hungry, but what does the devil do? He tempts Jesus to turn stones into bread. This is the temptation that appeals to the lust of the flesh. On the pinnacle: The temptation to show off. This is the temptation that appeals to the pride of life (fame). On a high mountain: Where a person sees what's available. This is the temptation that appeals to the lust of the eyes. Often times we boast about our senses, but that's also where the devil tempts us. Let's be real, the trouble that we've gotten into in our lives had something to do with either our eyes, ears, nose, hands, or our tongues. To win the battle against Satan we must not yield to temptation. We all will be tempted, but we all don't have to yield to temptations. *"There is no temptation taken you, but such as is common to man, but God is faithful, who will not suffer you to be tempted above that you are able, but with the temptation also make a way to escape, that you may be able to bear it"* (1 Corinthians 10:13). That's good news! Think about it. All of us will be tempted at some point. However, we have a God that cares so much about us that he tempers our temptations, and also gives us a way out in the midst of our temptations. What a mighty God we serve!

The third enemy is what the Bible calls the "flesh" or our sinful nature. Every single one of us has to deal with the flesh, no matter how long we've known the Lord, and no matter how spiritual we may be. If we would be honest our flesh is against us. We have to daily kill our fleshly desires and habits. If not, they will destroy us. Again, Paul declares in Romans 7, that there is no "*good thing*" in his flesh. That's why the Spirit of God is so necessary in the life of the believer. What he's saying is that because of his flesh (his nature) he's unable to please God as he should. Paul admits that his flesh is working against him. Look at what he says in verses 19-21. *"For the good that I would I do not: but the evil which I would not, that I do. Now if I do that I would not, it is no more I that do it, but sin that dwelleth in me. I find then a law, that, when I would do good, evil is present with me."*

There is a constant battle going on within us. The flesh against the Spirit. Be it assured, when Paul says that evil is present with him, he's not speaking of someone else. We have the same struggles and battles that the Apostle Paul had. Honestly, I struggle every day not to give Satan victory when it comes to my flesh. I've learned that if we're to be victorious, we must subdue (bring under subjection) our sinful desires, thoughts and behaviors daily.

Daily communion with Christ helps us to overcome sin in our lives. The more we pray, meditate on His Word, and seek Him, the less we involve ourselves in sinful practices. I have found that the more I'm in the Word and in prayer, the easier it is for me to give the devil a black eye. We're stronger when we pray and meditate on the Word of God. Again, since all of us have the capacity to do wrong, it's easier to do right when we involve ourselves in God's Word and allow His Holy Spirit to saturate our hearts.

Pastor R. Covington Sr.

Chapter Four

Hanging On By The Threads

Rope is a flexible line made of fibers or wires twisted or braided together for tensile strength. Growing up as a child on the Westside of Indianapolis in a neighborhood called Haughville, we didn't have very much, but we had each other. I remember climbing what we called cigar trees in our back yard. We would climb the trees and tie what we called Tarzan ropes on the limbs to hold us when we climbed up or swung on the trees. The ropes had to be at least two inches in diameter. Actually, as I remember, it consisted of about three ropes intertwined or braided together to form one rope. I was so used to climbing and holding onto that rope in my backyard that when I went to gym in junior high school, I had no problem holding onto the rope when we had to climb. During that time, I had no fears or reservations while holding onto the rope. Reason being, I knew in my mind and heart that not only was the rope strong enough to hold me, but what the rope was tied to could hold me. For years there was no doubt in my mind that I was hanging onto faith and that my faith was tied to a living and loving God. I remember my roots during my mail carrying days, in which I would stop at some of my customer's houses to pray with some of the ones that I knew were sick. I had enough faith to believe that if I prayed for them, God would heal them. I remember on one occasion one of my customer's husband was having a seizure and his wife called me in to pray for him. I read Scripture and as I started praying and asking "In Jesus Name," her husband began to calm down and came to himself. Man that was a boost for my faith! Honestly, I felt like I had "mountain moving faith." That moment stayed with me for years to come, but suddenly all of that changed. In one night and the days that followed, I went from holding onto the strong rope of faith, to hanging on by the threads. All of the faith I thought I had wasn't there. The fibers were falling away moment by moment, hour by hour and day by day. I felt like I could no longer hold on. I actually wanted to give in and give up. I wanted to throw in the towel. I felt like the Prophet Jeremiah when he stated in Jeremiah 20:9, *"Then I said, I will not make mention of him, nor speak anymore in His name."* I couldn't understand why God allowed this to happen. During this moment, I found myself still constantly trying to wake up from this dream, or should I say nightmare. If there ever was a time that I needed my mother, it was then. For most of my life, I always knew there were two people who I could call on whenever I needed help, God and my mother. To me, Mrs. Aline Scott Covington was the strongest person in the world. She had what I believe was the faith of Abraham. The problem was she had gone to be with the Lord that she had led us to. She was the strong anchor of the family. She showed strength and encouragement to us during the hard and tragic times when she didn't have anybody physically to encourage her. It was absolutely amazing how she was able to endure the passing of her mother and the murder of her second born son without complaining or compromising her faith. She stood as only a woman of extreme faith could do, and tell us that we have to put our trust in God. I truly know now through experience how my mother made it day by day. I know what helped me to hang on, even though I was hanging onto threads. Besides prayer, I learned that sometimes you have to encourage yourself. I also learned that during some of the most hardest times, some of the people who you thought would be there for you and with you, are nowhere to be found. Or if they are, they are miserable comforters. Remember Job's story that we talked about in chapter one, how Job lost everything, but held onto his integrity. His three what I call so-called friends, were there with him, but not for him. Believe this, everybody that is with you may not be for you! Eliphaz, Bildad and Zophar were there with Job, but when you read the text, you see that they sat at a distance and just looked at him. For seven days and nights, they stared at him and didn't say a mumbling word. They didn't say anything but they were thinking, and their thinking brought them to the same conclusion. Job must have done something wrong to be in this shape. God is punishing him for his sins. I've discovered that some people just don't know what to say. Then there are others who don't have to say anything. Their expression says it all. Many times, there are those who have what I call the "Uh Hum" Syndrome. In other words' "Now it's coming out," we know you did something to wind up this way. When you keep reading you find that discourse after discourse Job has to respond to these attacks. Eventually, in Chapter 16, he tells those so-called friends, *"my witness is in heaven and my record on high."* Halleluiah! God keeps good records.

During this tragic time people (Christians) were saying, "Don't blame yourself," actually I didn't. We are not responsible for what our children do. I already knew that. "You're the pastor, you've got to be strong." It was like I was supposed to ignore the fact that my son was in pain and facing the death penalty or the pain that all the families involved were in. I think one of the mistakes that we make in life as pastors, preachers and men and women of God is to put or allow someone else to put a big "S" on our chest. I must confess, I'm not faster than a speeding bullet, nor am I more powerful than a locomotive. I am not able to leap tall buildings in a single bound, I'm not Superman! And you must realize, no matter what people say, neither are you. Some didn't say anything, but their looks and stares said it all. People knew how we were being blessed as a church and family. People knew my son from infancy and knew of his caring and loving spirit. They witnessed his mannerly disposition. They saw how he cared and supported his children, yet some succumbed to that same judgmental spirit that Job's so-called friends had. At that time, I felt like there were those that thought I should turn my back on my son. Yes, he messed up terribly, but he was and is still my son. I love him just as much and more today. That night he realized that he had made the biggest mistake of his life. I was there. I felt his hurt. I felt his sorrow. I felt his pain. I felt his love for his family, particularly his children. That same night we cried, prayed, and hugged. The days ahead would not get easier. At this point, I already felt horrible and had no energy. The situation had zapped my strength. I was ready to throw in the towel. I didn't feel like or even want to go to church. I couldn't bring myself to stand in the pulpit and preach God's Word. The last thing I needed was the congregation looking to see what I would do, or how I would react. I already knew, if I had to stand, there would be no preaching from me, as I could hardly pray. All I felt like doing is what I had been doing. Crying! I really didn't need any miserable comforters. I thank God for a supportive family and for the most part a supporting church. During this difficult time and in the weeks after, some of my true preacher friends were there for whatever I needed. For that I'm eternally grateful. In the midst of all of this, one thing is certain, it doesn't matter what you're going through or what people are saying about you, God has a record! He knows all and sees all. He knows all the circumstances.

Actually, there are some people, who mean well, but just don't know what to say. However, on the other hand, there are also some people who are just mean. That's the very reason why you have to sometimes encourage yourself. In 1st Samuel 30, David, a man after God's own heart, had to do that very thing, encourage himself. He was distressed and depressed by problems in his life. David not only had problems, but also was in a position where he had no one to turn to but the Lord. Moreover, that's just what David did. He encouraged himself in the Lord, which meant he strengthened himself in the Lord. Beloved, we must understand that sometimes God allows us or puts us in a position where we are alone and have no choice but to turn to Him. So how do we at our lowest point, encourage or strengthen ourselves? First, we have to realize that the Lord is the source of our strength. There are some things that may make us feel better (drugs, alcohol, or even other people) but they can't give us strength from within. Secondly, we have to get into God's Word. When everything else and everybody else leaves you, God's Word will be there. Jesus states in Matthew 24:35, *"heaven and earth shall pass away, but my Word shall not pass away."* God's Word will be there when you need it. We pass up a great opportunity when we neglect to read, study and meditate on God's Word. The writer of Hebrews 4:12 says, *"for the Word of God is living and active....* (NIV). The Word of God is not only living but it energizes. Sometimes the only thing that gets me going and picks me up is God's Word. The living Word of God is food for our souls. It reveals God's will for our lives. When we open our minds and our hearts to its speaking and revelation, it refreshes, strengthens and transforms us. The Word of God is not only food for our souls, but the Psalmist says, *"it was a lamp unto his feet, a light unto his path."* Listen, we need the Word of God to make it through this dark world. Be careful not to minimize the Word of God in your life. It has all the answers to all of life's situations. Third, if we are to be strengthened, we must draw from history. We must draw from what God has already done in our lives. All of us have had some previous experiences that we know without God we would not have made it. Often times God allows us to have victories, and to win battles, so that we will have something to draw from for the next battle. David experienced this when he was about to face the giant Goliath. In 1st Samuel 17, David shows his trust in God, *"David said moreover, The LORD that delivered me out of the paw of the lion, and out of the paw of the bear, he will deliver me out of the hand of this Philistine. And Saul said unto David, Go, and the LORD be with thee"* (1Samuel 17:37).

Sometimes God also uses the trials in our life to prepare us for something greater in ministry. They help to develop our confidence. They teach us lessons that we probably would have never learned if trials had never came our way. I appreciate that traditional song, *"Through It All."* Truly, I have learned over the years, that instead of getting angry with God, concerning our trails, we ought to thank Him. First, we ought to thank Him for bringing us through, next, for using our trails to teach and perfect us.

Finally, if we are to be strengthened, we must deepen our intimacy with God. Intimacy is defined as, "a close, familiar, and usually affectionate or loving personal relationship with another person or group." Intimacy doesn't just happen overnight. It's a process and it takes time. Spending time with God is a privilege and brings about intimacy. It's a sad truth, but if we are honest, we spend the most time with God when we are going through something or when tragedy confronts us. When things are going well with us, when everything seems to be going in the right direction, we seem to forget about the God that has made things well or has kept things going in the right direction for us. We acquire the same syndrome as the Children of Israel did, Spiritual Amnesia! I believe God was also talking to us when he challenged Israel as they were about to enter Canaan.

10 When thou hast eaten and art full, then thou shalt bless the LORD thy God for the good land which he hath given thee. 11Beware that thou forget not the LORD thy God, in not keeping his commandments, and his judgments, and his statutes, which I command thee this day: 12 Lest when thou hast eaten and art full, and hast built goodly houses, and dwelt therein; 13 And when thy herds and thy flocks multiply, and thy silver and thy gold is multiplied, and all that thou hast is multiplied; 14 Then thine heart be lifted up, and thou forget the LORD thy God, which brought thee forth out of the land of Egypt, from the house of bondage; 15 Who led thee through that great and terrible wilderness, wherein were fiery serpents, and scorpions, and drought, where there was no water; who brought thee forth water out of the rock of flint; [16] Who fed thee in the wilderness with manna, which thy fathers knew not, that he might humble thee, and that he might prove thee, to do thee good at thy latter end; [17] And thou say in thine heart, My power and the might of mine hand hath gotten me this wealth. [18] But thou shalt remember the LORD thy God: for it is he that giveth thee power to get wealth, that he may establish his covenant which he sware unto thy fathers, as it is this day. Deuteronomy 8:10-18 (KJV)

Beloved, nothing takes the place of spending time with God, NOTHING! Not silver or gold, houses or land, nor people or places. There's nothing that can truly satisfy our souls but God. I've been there. I've had money, a good job, material possessions, and other people in my life. None of these things or people can replace intimacy with God. Intimacy doesn't come with just a head knowledge of God. In the natural, birth occurs when intimacy has taken place. It's the same spiritually. God wants to birth something in all of us. Where there is intimacy, God can birth healing, comfort and peace in any situation. Again, intimacy comes from spending quality and quantity time with God.

We spend time with God by studying and meditating on His Word. We spend time with God through prayer. Every believer can have intimacy with God through fellowship. Fellowship in the Greek is (Koinonia), which carries two meanings, partnership and participation. In the book of James, we are told to, *"draw near to God and He will draw near to us"* (James 4:8). This is not a, if you want to thing, this is a command to us from God.

In Philippians 3:10 Paul says, *"That I may know him, and the power of his resurrection, and the fellowship of his sufferings, being made conformable unto his death."* In this verse, Paul is emphasizing knowing Christ in a personal way. He doesn't just want to know about Him, he wants to know Him. He wants and we should also want to have an intimate knowledge of Jesus Christ. To many Christians are satisfied with having salvation, and that's it. But, that's not enough. Salvation guarantees our going to heaven, but an intimate knowledge of Jesus Christ makes the trip much better. We as believers must take the time to grow in our knowledge of Jesus Christ. Paul's conviction and ambition was to know

Him [Christ] personally. That should also be our conviction and ambition.

Again, Paul says, *"that I may know HIM!"* Paul had a desire to personally know the Lord Jesus Christ. He doesn't say that he wanted to know about Him, because everybody knows about Him. Even the devil knows about Jesus.

Intimacy builds trust! It's hard to fully trust someone that you don't know. Intimacy with God makes Proverbs 3:5-6 a reality in the life of believers even when we don't understand what's going on in our life. We'll discuss this in a later chapter. It's not enough to know God with our head, we must know Him with our heart. Intimacy doesn't just happen.

Chapter Five

What Do You Do When You Don't Know What To Do?

As I was growing up, I was fortunate to play little league baseball on a team called the Cubs. I make this statement that I was fortunate because I really couldn't play. I was just friends with one of the coach's son, so they let me on the team. I couldn't hit the ball because I was scared of the ball. I played left field, but I never caught a ball, because I couldn't judge where the ball was going. I really didn't enjoy playing, but I did enjoy going to eat after each game. As I grew up, I really didn't get into watching baseball except during the World Series. One of the things that was interesting to me was how the pitcher could throw the ball with such precision. How he could be looking side to side or in back of himself and still throw the ball where he needed it to go, striking the opposing players out. I noticed something as I was watching a baseball game one night. The pitcher was getting ready to throw the ball, and as he threw the ball it went straight for the batter. All of a sudden the ball that was going straight took a curve. All I could say was Wow! That's how it's done. Then I thought about it, that's the way life is. The very sport that is least on my list, taught me a great lesson. Everything in life can be going straight but suddenly can take a curve. Often times when this happens, and if we are honest, we don't know what to do. We've got the questions but we don't have the answers. It's at this time when you have those who mean well, but offer you some generic answers. Here you are, broken hearted, hurt, down and out. You feel like you have lost everything that matters to you. You're ready to give up. Your dream has turned into a nightmare, and the only thing somebody has to say is, "don't worry, it's going to be alright. You know the Bible says, God won't put no more on you that you're able to bear," and honestly, you're not feeling that. You put on a fake smile and say thank you, but on the inside you're saying, "I already knew that, tell me something I don't know. I know it's going to be alright, but what do I do until alright happens. I have discovered that you can know the Word, be saved, be in church, have the church in you and still not know what to do. I've been there, you've been there. Things can happen so fast and so bad that all of your education, all of your ingenuity and ability can't help you.

Honestly, on this terrible night I didn't know what to do. All of my Bible College and Seminary training didn't prepare me to handle this situation. I know I'm saved and a child of God, but I was surrounded by circumstances that I had no control over. In 2nd Chronicles 20, Jehosophat finds himself in that situation, spiritual and surrounded. Surrounded by enemies that had joined forces to fight against him. The text lets us know that Jehosophat became fearful, frightened, and fainthearted. In verse 12 he tells God, *"We have no power to face this vast army that is attacking us, and we don't know what to do."* Beloved, the question for us is, what do you do when you don't know what to do? First, the text encourages us to "Seek God." Even though we don't know what to do, we ought to know where to turn. Often times when things happen we turn from God and church, but turn to alcohol, drugs, people that can't help us, and false securities. I want to encourage you. Whatever you might be going through, whether it be a drug or alcoholic condition, a marriage that's on the brink of divorce, sickness, death or whatever, Seek God!

Pastor R. Covington Sr.

Turn to Him. Isaiah 55:6 encourages us to *"Seek the LORD while he may be found; call on him while he is near."* You need to know that God loves you and honestly, there are children of God in church that love you also.

Secondly, fast and pray! Jesus told His disciples on an occasion that some things come only by fasting and praying. Fasting puts things in the right perspective. It says that food and things in life are not as important to me as my relationship with God. Fasting and prayer go together like peanut butter and jelly. Fasting is abstaining while prayer is appealing. When we pray we're letting God know that we are dependent on Him.

Thirdly, keep your eyes on the Lord. Jehosophat tells God that he doesn't know what to do, but his eyes are on Him. Sometimes we let our circumstances cause us to focus on circumstances and not on Christ. I heard somebody say, "don't focus on how big your problem is, focus on how big God is." Listen, whenever we take our eyes off Jesus we set ourselves up for a fall. Just ask Peter, who in Matthew 14, he is walking on water until he takes his eyes off Jesus and puts them on the storm that has confronted him. The text says, *"But when he saw the wind boisterous, he was afraid; and beginning to sink, he cried, saying, Lord, save me. And immediately Jesus stretched forth his hand, and caught him, and said unto him, O thou of little faith, wherefore didst thou doubt?"* Looking at this we can criticize Peter, but I believe we have to give him some credit. He did take his focus off of the Master, but when he began to sink, he had enough faith and humility to ask for help. Even Jesus said he had little faith, and a little faith is better than no faith. When the facts say one thing our faith ought to kick in and say and do something else.

Real faith is not just something you say.
Real faith is not just something you feel.
Real faith is not just something you think.
Real faith is not just something you believe.
Real faith is something you do.

Lastly, when you don't know what to do, don't be afraid or have too much ego and pride to ask for help. While going through this ordeal there were times when I just didn't know what to do. Honestly, I find myself in that same situation at times now. What I learned was, that I had to realize and be truthful about where I was. I was in a place that I had never been. How could I know what to do? The problem for me was that I was concerned about what people would think. After all, I'm a PASTOR. I can't let people see my frailty. I'm suppose to have the answers to give to people when they come to me. Listen, people need to see our humanity. They need to know that we don't have all the answers. Whatever profession or field you are in, whether pastor, preacher, teacher, father, mother, etc., you need to know and people need to know that you have the same pains and problems that they have. You bleed red blood also. You have emotions just as they do. Yes, by all means, talk to God. He knows exactly what you're going through, but know also that He has placed people around you who can empathize, sympathize and be compassionate with you. Pray for discernment, because you can't talk to everybody, and you don't want to talk to everybody, particularly somebody that has never been through anything. I'm going to be honest. I really had to pray for myself and some people after I talked with them and after they gave me their one cent. I had to get my attitude and spirit right. At that moment, I didn't need to hear all about how well their children were getting along and all the good things that they were doing, and how they had never gave them trouble. This wasn't about them. I needed to hear "I don't understand all that has happened, but I'm praying for you." "I haven't been where you are, but I know God is going to help you through it." "I'm praying for you, your son, and your family." Eventually, after getting over the conversation, I began to get my thoughts back on the right side of the road. I had to do this because my flesh was beginning to take over. For a moment, I was thinking "just wait," but I found myself praying that they or anyone would never have to experience what I was going through. When you don't know what to do: Seek God! Fast and Pray! Keep your eyes on the Lord, and lastly, don't be afraid to ask for help.

Chapter Six

I Can't Figure It Out (Proverbs 3:5-6)

Trust in the LORD with all thine heart; and lean not unto thine own understanding. In all thy ways acknowledge him, and he shall direct thy paths.

As I had stated in an earlier chapter, I had a problem understanding why God would allow such a tragedy to happen in my family. Years later, I'm doing better but I still haven't yet figured it out. I always knew that there would be some things that would happen in life that we won't have the answers to or an understanding of. I believe that because of our humanity and our frailty, we will always have questions that we desire to be answered. Even in that moment, we still have to put our trust in God. Yes, it's easier saying than doing, because I don't know anybody who likes to live in the sphere of the unknown. It's like going around in the darkness, which for most people is uncomfortable. I was there, in the midst of confusion, wandering around in the darkness of not understanding and trying to figure out what happened. I was in a place where I had never been. I couldn't make sense of anything.

Pastor R. Covington Sr.

I remember one day, I was driving to a church on the south side of Indianapolis. When I arrived there, it was daylight outside. By the time, the benediction was given and we were leaving, it had gotten dark. As I was driving home, I took a wrong turn and eventually found myself in a place that I wasn't familiar with nor comfortable with. Frustration crept in because of three things. First, it was dark and I didn't know where I was, which actually I did. Lost! Next, I couldn't figure how I got there, and last I didn't know how I was going to find my way to familiar surroundings. I drove around and around getting more frustrated by the minute and by the dead ends that I kept driving into. Then I finally saw something. I saw the lighting from the downtown area. I knew then that all I would have to do is to keep my eyes on the light that was coming from down town and I would eventually be where I needed to be.

Going through this tragedy in the earlier days, I was lost, confused, in darkness trying to make sense of what was going on. Nothing I thought about made sense. I couldn't understand it, and I couldn't figure it out. But, I knew that if I was going to get through this, I had to put and keep my trust in God. God is the light that led me to where I am now, trusting in God. In Proverbs 3:5-6, there are two key truths that arise. Number one, when you can't figure it out you must, trust the Lord completely. In verse 5 Solomon says, *"trust in the Lord."* Trust means to have confidence, to confide in. Trust is a dependence on somebody or something. One of the problems with so many people is that they trust, but their trust is centered on the wrong person or thing. It's dangerous to put your total trust in something or someone other than God. The Psalmist in Psalms 118:8 says, *"it's better to trust in the Lord than to put confidence in man."* Trusting God means you rely more on the unseen than on the seen. You may not believe it, but the unseen is more powerful than the seen. Think about it, the wind, you can't see, but we know it's there because we can feel it blowing. We can't see it, but we know it's there because of it's action. Think about your breath, you can't see it, but it moves in and out of your lungs through our mouths and noses.

The story is told of a Christian man who worked in a factory. One day one of his co-workers came up to him and said, "why are you always talking about a God that you can't see? How do you know if he is really real?" The Christian man said, "yes, you are right, we can't see Him, but let me ask you a few questions." He says to him, "have you ever seen or heard a pain?" The man answered, "no". Again he asked him, "have you ever smelled pain?" The man answered, "no". Finally, the Christian man said, "well if you have never heard, seen or smelled pain, how do you know that there is pain?" The man responded, "because I can feel it." The events of that night took me to a place where I needed more than something that I could see. That night as numb as I was, I needed to feel the presence of God.

When we struggle to trust in God, we tend to put our trust in something else, or someone, including ourselves. Trusting God means that He has all (100%) of our heart. A divided heart is almost as bad as having no trust at all. When we really trust God, we relinquish ownership of all of our problems, worries and situations. In other words, we give them to God. We put them all in His hands. We do that because He can handle every one of our problems, worries and situations. We must trust God completely. Too many times, we say we have given this and that to God when we really haven't. When we really trust God

Pastor R. Covington Sr.

completely, we stop trying to help Him out. Indeed, it's a growing process. The truth is, most of us don't get there over night. I can remember time and time again, when I actually thought I had put a problem in the Lord's hand, only to realize that I was still trying to co-pilot with God. The truth is, when I really relinquished my problem to Him, He handled it.

Not only should we trust God with all of our heart, but we must not depend on our own ingenuity. Solomon says for us *"not to lean to our own understanding."* When we lean to our own understanding, it means we are relying on our own limited viewpoint and reasoning. As much as we want to, we can't see it all or know it all. We aren't omniscient or omnipotent. That attribute belongs only to God and not us. Solomon tells us, *"lean not to thy own understanding."* When we cannot figure it out, we must lean on the Lord. In the physical realm it's impossible to lean on your own self. (Try it and you will find yourself falling all the time). In the spiritual realm it's ineffectual to lean on yourself. When we really trust God, we acknowledge Him. When we acknowledge God, we recognize that He is our all-sufficient God. When we acknowledge God in all of our ways, then we're assured of His promise that He will direct our paths. I must confess that, had not the Lord directed my path and ordered my every step, I wouldn't be writing this book today.

Years have passed, and I still haven't figured everything out. Things are still cloudy, but I trust God, and know that beyond the clouds the sun will shine. I am reminded of the time that I was preparing to go to West Virginia to attend the National Baptist Congress of Christian Education. I had never flown on airplane, and of course I was nervous. No, I was scared as, I've always had a fear of heights. As I arrived at the airport, not only did the fear escalate, but it started to rain outside. By the time I boarded the plane, it was raining harder, and the skies were getting darker. When I arrived at my seat, to my surprise, I had a window seat. Eventually the plane started taking off down the runway. By this time, not only was it raining and dark, but it began thundering and lightning. As the plane gained altitude, all I could see looking out the window, was that it was getting darker, it was raining much harder, and the thunder and lightning was increasing. The plane was going higher when all of the sudden the pilot got on the speaker and said, "we are about to go into a storm and we have to gain altitude." Now I'm really scared! The plane was gaining altitude, and all I'm seeing and hearing is lightning and thundering. As I'm looking out the window, suddenly the pilot guides the plane through and above the clouds. To my amazement, the sun was shining. Wow! I couldn't believe it. It was storming down below, but above the clouds, the sun was shining. Listen, you might be going through a storm right now, but trust God and allow Him to take you above your circumstances. It took me a while to grasp this, but while I'm trying to figure it out, God is already working it out, and I know now, that the sun will shine after a while.

Pastor R. Covington Sr.

Chapter Seven

Can't Win for Loosing

Years have passed since this horrible night happened, but for me, in the words of the great poet Langston Hughes, *"Life Ain't Been No Crystal Stair. It's had tacks in it, and splinters, and boards torn up. And places with no carpet on the floor—Bare."* There I was. There I am. There I was. Growing up in a family of all boys, we couldn't help but be competitive. Winning was what we did, even though we did lose from time to time, because we did the same things day after day. It was nothing for us to be playing basketball, ping-pong or shooting pool after we got out of school on the weekdays and from morning until night on weekends and during the summer. As the years would come and go I found myself from time to time on the winning side. I won basketball tournaments. I won an election to become the President of a Community Organization among other things. I was winning in life more than I was losing, but then all of a sudden, I found myself in a place that I didn't like to be in or wanted to be in. Losing more than I was winning. I don't know anybody that likes to lose all the time. It was frustrating and at times infuriating. I couldn't understand what was going on, or why it was going on. After all, as Christians aren't we suppose to win? I know I'm saved and was trying to do the right thing for the right reasons. As weeks and months went by I was at a total lost. No matter what I tried to do when it came to my son and his children, I found myself on the losing end and fighting a losing battle. In my heart, I felt and still feel as if the courts cared nothing about the welfare of my grandchildren. They were only interested in retrying my son repeatedly, even though he was already serving time. I was treated as if I had committed a crime, by an unjust system and others who took advantage because they had the advantage. Evil forces were at work and my grandchildren were right in the middle of a struggle that they had not caused. As I fought and fought to try and give my grand-children a better life, and to stop certain non-blood relatives from taking their names, it soon became evident again that I was losing another battle. Well, eventually I lost again. I lost all custody. Not only could the children not visit their father in prison, but also the other relatives did all they could to turn the children against their father. Eventually, they took my grandchildren's last name from them. When it came to losing, I really lost it. They just took my grandchildren's name. At that moment, I thought about the movie documentary "*Roots*" and how they took Kunta Kenta's name. It hurt even more because I felt that they tried to make sure that there would no longer be a Ronald Covington III. Again, I felt that all of this was done out of an evil spirit just to hurt my son and myself. Well they succeeded. I hurt and it still hurts to a certain degree. I have to admit, I was angry with everybody including myself. I couldn't understand what I was doing wrong. So again I began to rehearse those same thoughts in my head. Why was I losing every battle? Again, I found myself thinking, all my life I had tried to be a good person and help others. I have always gave more than I would get. I know I'm saved and on the Lord's side so what is really going on? I found myself in a place that I knew God, my mother, and really myself, would not want me to be in. I knew what the Bible said, but if there ever was a time that I wanted revenge, it was now. If there ever was a time that I wanted to hurt (somebody) because I was hurt, it was now. At that time I knew then and I felt then, the realness in that old adage, "hurt people, hurt people." When we're hurt, we naturally want to strike back. We want to hurt those who are hurting us. I know that in certain circumstances, people who are hurt often times hurt others without being aware of it. This is because of the hurt and pain that has been inflicted on them, and without even thinking about it, they inflict hurt onto somebody else, and not the person who has hurt them. Over the years as a pastor, I've had to council couples where one party has been hurt in a previous relationship and unknowingly brought that hurt to their present relationship. Repeatedly, I heard the same story, different people. I'm not his ex! Or I'm not her ex! One partner without realizing it was hurting their partner because they had been hurt in their past relationship. I have to admit, I wasn't in that category of not being aware of wanting to hurt someone. I was hurting and I wanted to retaliate. I know hate is a strong word, but if there ever was a time when I came close to hating someone, it was then. Honestly, I wanted God to do something, and not just do something, but do something for me. I wanted Him to condescend to my level and do what I had in mind. I was sick and tired of being sick and tired of losing. I was truly in a war for my soul. As I had talked about in chapter three, there was a constant battle going on between my flesh and my spirit. At this point, the flesh was winning. I can't pretend and act like everything was well with my soul, because it wasn't. Yes, I was pastoring Friendship Missionary Baptist Church located in Indianapolis, Indiana, and I still am. I was preaching and teaching, and I still am. Nevertheless, I was also human, and I'm still human. I found myself in a low place where I had to seek council from the Word of God. I found refuge in Psalm 37, where the Psalmist David writes concerning an age old problem concerning why the righteous suffer and the wicked seem to prosper. I know for myself and others, that we are thankful for the Omniscient God, that breathed on David to write this Psalm of encouragement. He knew that some of us would be where Asaph was in the 73rd Psalms, and would need something outside of ourselves to help us. In this Psalms Asaph says, *"But as for me, I almost lost my footing. My feet were slipping, and I was almost gone. For I envied the proud when I saw them prosper despite their wickedness."* If the truth be told, so many times we lose focus, because of "stuff" that's going on around us, and we allow it to get inside of us. Therefore, David writes this 37th Psalms to urge us to have patience and put our trust in God. When we read the text, this is not the young shepherd boy David that slew a lion, bear and a Philistine giant named Goliath, but this is the David who has gone through many years of experience. This is the same David who writes in the 23rd Psalms, *"The Lord is my Shepherd, I shall not want,"* but now writes in this 37th Psalms, *"I have been young, but now I'm old, yet I have never seen the righteous forsaken, nor his seed begging bread."* In this 37th Psalm, David encourages us to have confidence in God, in spite of and in the midst of our condition. Not only does David encourage us, but he also instructs us. He gives us two negative instructions and four positive instructions. He tells us what not to do, and then turns around and tells us what to do. The first thing he says is, *"Fret not thyself because of evil doers."* When David uses the word "FRET" he is speaking about more than just worrying. David is really saying don't get overly angry and heated up. In our modern day, young people's vernacular, David is saying "Chill Out". He says *"Fret not"*, but then he says, *"don't be envious."* Beloved, when we envy, we compare ourselves to someone else who has what we want. The problem comes in that they may have what we want, but not what we need. And watch this! if we spend all of our time focusing on the evil doers and workers of iniquity, it will not only be wasted time but we will take the chance of missing out on the blessings that God has in store for us. We have to be very careful, for anger and envy can blind us to the point, that we begin to walk in the way that seems right, but in the end is destruction (Proverbs 14:12). All because we want something that doesn't belong to us, "**Revenge**". We don't have that right, and when we think we do. We are really telling God, I don't trust you to do what you said you would do. God said in Romans 12:19, *"Vengeance is mine, I will repay."* The question is, will we trust God or not? Or will we allow the situation to dictate whether we will or not?

Listen to me! Too many times, we lose focus and allow somebody to have control over us without us even realizing it. I've been there. I had to think about it and challenge myself. Why am I allowing this insignificant person to have this much control over my thoughts and my desires. They are **NOT** that important. They have nothing whatsoever to do with me living, moving, and having my being. It took me a while, but I finally got it. The devil had me just where he wanted me, thinking like he thinks and wanting to do what he would do. I was allowing my circumstances to take control over me, causing me to get overly angry. I had to really concentrate on not allowing Satan to have his way in my life. If I was to overcome this momentary lapse, I would not only have to put into practice the "do-nots" of Psalms 37, but I would also have to do what was right, even though I felt wronged. After all, what we have to understand is that, we don't have to give an account for what someone does to us, but we do have to give an account, and are held responsible, for our response to them. David gives us two negative disciplines when he says, fret not thyself and neither be envious, but he also gives us four positive disciplines. The first thing he says is, "*Trust in the Lord.*" He leaves no room for questioning or debate concerning who we ought to trust in. I believe he does this because there are times when we put our trust in somebody or something other than God. I believe also that David is saying that we ought to trust

God no matter what the circumstances might be, because if we are honest, sometimes we let our surrounding circumstances control the thermostat of our faith. David says that we ought to trust in the Lord. To trust the Lord means to put your confidence and security in Him. When we really trust God, we depend upon His Providence, His Power and His Promise, for our protection and provision. When I was coming up in church, we use to sing a song called *"All In His Hands."* When we were singing that song, we were talking about God's hands. God's hands are not like our hands, but we speak in anthropomorphic terms, which mean to ascribe human form to deity. Does God have hands? Yes, and it's good to know that even in this twenty-first century that God's hands have not changed. They are just as powerful as they have always been. Whatever problems, burdens, circumstances or situations that we may have, we can put them all in God's hands. And beloved, I know this. The only reason why I am still here today is because I am in His hands. It's good to know that whatever is going on in our life, we can take it out of our hands, and put it in the Lord's hand. God has big hands, and if He can hold the whole world in His hands, surely He can handle our problems. David not only says, "*trust in the Lord,*" but he also says, "do *good.*" When David says, "do *good*", it's in the imperative voice, which means it's a command. God is not giving us a choice. We've got to do good even when others are doing bad. In other words, we must keep doing what is right while we are waiting on God. In the context of the text, some of God's people were tempted to leave the land, which was equivalent to saying that God wasn't faithful and couldn't be trusted. David says do good right where you are, trust God for what you need and God will bless you. I found out long ago, that if you have a problem within yourself, allowing external situations to affect us internally, leaving won't make the situation go away. It goes wherever you go. So we might as well stay where we are and receive the benefits of God's blessing.

Life can really be tough. Honestly, conflicts, complications and the cares of this world, if we allow, will rob us of our joy, suck the life out of us, and finally leave us feeling helpless and hopeless. Again, I've been there, but thank God, He lets us know how to counter these feelings. He says to us, "*delight thyself also in the Lord and Find your pleasure, peace, and prosperity in Me."* Once we determine that our happiness will not be determined by what happens, we are on our way to greater things. The Psalmist says, if we delight ourselves in the Lord, He will give us the desires of our hearts (Psalms 37:4). Now, let us not look and interpret this verse in the wrong manner, because we have to be careful, not to let our circumstances darken our desires or harden our hearts. What David is saying is, when we delight ourselves in the Lord, then God will give us what is truly desirable and good for us. We need to understand that God can never and will never be a partner to evil, sinful and selfish desires. Our desires must line up with the will and Word of the Lord.

David also challenges us to commit our way unto the Lord (Psalm 37:5). Beloved, even when things are not going our way, we cannot have our way. We have to be willing to surrender our way and turn our life over to God and let Him have His way. I'm the first to admit that this isn't easy. You want to lash out and get somebody, but when you truly commit your way unto the Lord, your way is not as important as God's way. Finally, those of us who have been hurt by other people, need to forgive if they want to be set free. No matter what the circumstances are, we are obligated and commanded to forgive. The truth is, nobody deserves or earns forgiveness, it must be granted. Thank God, that He doesn't forgive us based on our deserving it, because if that was the case, we would all still be doomed to the wages of sin. Our forgiveness from God is based on His love and mercy for us. Again, there is nothing we can do or say to deserve forgiveness, so we must forgive. Is it easy? No, especially when it's the same person inflicting the hurt, but we don't have a choice. If we want God to forgive us, we must forgive others. Forgiveness is not only a command, but it is also a choice. When we choose not to forgive, we choose to remain prisoners of our past. We choose to have our prayer life affected. Really? Yes! Psalms 66:18 says, *"If I regard iniquity in my heart, the Lord will not hear me."* In other words, if God has convicted us about some sin in our life, we know it but continue to sin, then our prayers are in vain. God does not even hear them. Beloved, unforgiveness is sin, and if we want God to hear us, we must choose to forgive. What we have to remember is that no matter how rough the mountain gets, how deep the valley is, God is still in control. When it seems like you can't win for losing, remember that with God, we are always on the winning side.

Chapter Eight
Where I Am Now and Where Am I Going From Here?

A few years have passed since that tragic evening that changed the lives of so many people. A lot has happened. There have been many ups and downs. I've lost more battles than I've won concerning this tragedy, but I'm still trusting God. Some of the days, weeks, months, and years have been tougher than others, but I know God has brought us and will continue to bring us through. I know I could not and would not have made it, if had not been for the presence of God, the love of family and the strength of my son who is still incarcerated. He helped me when he didn't even know he was helping me. The times when I would visit him, seeing him so strong, gave me strength. I actually was amazed at his strength. Here he was facing what he was facing, and still smiling, joking, and being himself. Nevertheless, that's who he's always been and what he has always done, looking out for others. I believe he knew in his heart that if he broke down, it would devastate me more. I think we had a secret pact unbeknown to each other, to be strong for each other. While visiting him, he never cried because he knew I would, and actually, I did, but not in front of him. I can remember many times driving home from the prison and tears would be flowing. However, not all of the tears were tears of sorrow. On some occasions, there were tears of joy. One particular occasion was when I took my son's children to see him. They had the most wonderful visit. When the visiting time was over, his children didn't want to leave and they were asking to come back again. All the way home, they were excited and anxious for the next visit. They were so full of joy and happiness that they were able to see their dad. However, in spite of how the children felt, that would be their last visit until all parties are in agreement concerning them visiting their father again. It will take some time to adjust, but we all know that the children will be of age to make their own decision.

Where am I now? Even though the threads have thickened, I must admit that I'm not where I'm going to be. I do know this. God has a way of turning things around, even when it seems that the odds are stacked against you. Even when you have waited and waited and it seems like God is not going to show up. He's done it before and I know He can do it again. I had to realize that God's delay is not always God's denial. In the eleventh chapter of the book of John, it seemed like the odds were stacked against Lazarus and his sisters Mary and Martha. With the human eye, and mindset, there was no hope for Lazarus, but Jesus turned his situation around. Often times if we are honest, things don't happen when we want them to happen. There are some in between times that are difficult and some, in between times that bother us. Some in between times when you know that God can, but He hasn't. How do you handle it when you are in between calling on the Lord and waiting for your answer? In between times when the promises of God are claimed, but not yet con-firmed. In the between time when you've prayed to God and now you're waiting on His presence, power, and provision. This can be a discouraging time, but I need to tell you that if you are here, you are not by yourself. Moses had an in between time and got discouraged in Numbers 11 because he was dealing with some complaining and murmuring from the Children of Israel, and asked God to kill him. Elijah had an in between time in 1st Kings when Jezebel threatened him and he asked God to take his life. Job had a moment after losing everything, and his so-called friends as the late Dr. Manuel Scott Sr. would say, "just looked him to death," for seven days and didn't say a mumbling word. Here in the book of John, Mary and Martha are having an in between moment because they sent for Jesus, but now they're waiting for Him to show up. Jesus is about a days' journey from Bethany when He gets word of His friend Lazarus being sick. I believe that all of us can identify with this because, the truth be known, all of us have been, and some of us are sick right now. Some are physically, mentally, and spiritually sick. Lazarus was sick! In his sickness, Mary and Martha summoned for the right person. There is a word for somebody here! Whatever you might be going through, things will get better if you get in touch with the right person, Jesus. I've had some things happen to me and nobody else could help me but the Lord. Yes, there have been times when I didn't have anyone else to call on, but I called on the Lord and got an answer.

Again, in John 11, notice how they summoned Jesus, without mentioning Lazarus's name. They just sent word and said, "*the one you love is sick.*" I like that because it's in the perfect tense, which means it portrays an action in progress. In other words, Lazarus is not himself, he is in a state of weakness, but the Lord still loves him. Even when I'm feeble, failing, and faltering, the Lord keeps on loving me. Even when I'm not myself, the Lord just keeps on loving me.

Secondly, they didn't make a certain request. They didn't ask the Lord for anything. They trusted the Lord for they knew that He knew what to do. They knew that He would do what was right. I must confess when I first read Jesus response in verse 4 it bothered me, because, in verse 4 He says, "*this sickness is not unto death*," but then I kept on reading, and in verse 14, he says, "*Lazarus is dead*." I had to go back to verse 4, and read it carefully. Jesus did say in verse 4, "*this sickness is not until death*," but He continues to say "*but for the glory of God, that the Son of God might be glorified thereby.*"

The Lord sees the other side of sickness. This sickness is for the glory of God. The text says, Jesus stayed where He was for two days. You would think that He would have got in a hurry when He got the news, but His delay was not his denial. Lazarus had been dead for four days, and rigor mortis had set in before Jesus arrived. Mary and Martha came to Jesus and said, *"if you had been here our brother would not have died."* Jesus tells them to show Him where they laid him. In spite of nature and time being at odds with Jesus, He said, *"show me where you laid him."* When Jesus arrived at Lazarus's grave, He prayed to His Father and told Lazarus to come forth (John 11:42). The text says, *"and he that was dead came forth, bound hand and foot with grave clothes, and his face was bound with a napkin."* Jesus said unto them. *"loose him and let him go."* Beloved, it's not over until God says it's over! If God can turn Lazarus situation around, He can surely turn ours around.

Where am I now? I'm in God's waiting room. What am I doing? Waiting on God. There is much in the Bible concerning us waiting on God, and if I can be honest, most of us don't like to wait. Society has gotten us in a mode where we're in a hurry and we want everything now. Road rage is at an epidemic level because we are in such a hurry. We live in a **microwave world**, because we are not willing to wait for our food to cook. Yes, waiting can be frustrating, and the waiting room is usually an uncomfortable place to be.

I remember the experience on most occasions of going to visit the doctor's office or clinic. I would first arrive and sign in. Then I would wait until they called my name to register me in. Next, they would call my name, sign me in and tell me to have a seat and wait until my name is called. Sounds familiar? Eventually a Medical Assistant would call me, take my weight, get my temperature and blood pressure and have me wait in another room for the doctor to come in. What makes this other room frustrating is first, you can't see what's going on outside the room. Secondly, you have no control of what's happening on the inside, and thirdly you don't know when the wait is going to be over. Beloved, we have to understand that waiting is not a matter of time it's a matter of faith and trust. We must believe that God knows where we are, and what we are feeling. Trust me, God knows us better than we know ourselves. He even knows us when we are anxious. I had to learn, and we all have to learn that God never has to hurry. He's always in control.

The psalmist in the 130th Psalms verse 1-2 says, *"Out of the depths have I cried unto thee, O LORD.*

Lord, hear my voice: let thine ears be attentive to the voice of my supplications," but in verse 5 he says, *"I wait for the LORD, my soul doth wait, and in his word do I hope."* In verses 1-2, the psalmist makes an earnest plea to the Lord. He knows that he is in a position that only God can handle. Moreover, that's the way it is in life at times. Things can and will happen to all of us that only God can do something about. There have been and will be times when we can cry out to no one but God. The psalmist takes his plea to God, but then he testifies that he was patiently waiting for the LORD. He compares his waiting to that of a city's watchmen. Therefore, I'm waiting and I'm watching for God to show Himself again. While I'm waiting, I'm just trusting, and consistently rehearsing in my spirit, Isaiah 40:29-31, *"He giveth power to the faint; and to them that have no might he increaseth strength. Even the youths shall faint and be weary, and the young men shall utterly fall: But they that wait upon the LORD shall renew their strength; they shall mount up with wings as eagles; they shall run, and not be weary; and they shall walk, and not faint."*

Where am I now?

I'm Hanging On!

Pastor R. Covington Sr.

Reference Page

Comparative Study Bible. (1999). Grands Rapids: Zondervan.

Dictionary.com. (2013). Retrieved from
http://dictionary.reference.com/

Hughes, L. (1994). Mother To Son. *Mother To Son.* Vintage Books.

Webster's Ninth New Collegiate Dictionary. (1989). Springfield: Merriam-Webster Inc.

About the Author

Pastor Ronald Covington Sr. is the senior Pastor of Friendship Missionary Baptist Church in Indianapolis, Indiana. In previous years, Pastor Covington has served on the Haughville Community Council, President of W.E.S.C.O. Community Organization, and Moderator of the Union District Baptist Association. He now serves as Vice President At Large of the General Missionary Baptist State Convention of Indiana Inc., and as a Board Member of the Equal Employment Opportunity Commission. He's also affiliated with the Ministers Alliance of Indiana and 10 Point Coalition.

Pastor Covington is the author of "*From the Pastor's Heart*"; a collection of devotionals, which initially began as emails sent to family, friends and members of Friendship inspired by his love and concern for others.

Pastor Covington is married to Sister Kim Covington and he is the father of four wonderful children, Ronald Jr., Rev. Rick, Rhea and Cameron.

Pastor R. Covington Sr.

Place An Order

Contact:

Friendship Missionary Baptist Church

1301 N. Goodlet Ave.

Indianapolis, Indiana 46222

Attention: Pastor Covington or Lakeiya Watson

Or

Amazon.com

www.howardpublishingpress.com

Thank you for supporting!

Pastor R. Covington Sr.

HOWARD PUBLISHING PRESS

Website: www.howardpublishing press.com
Email: howardpublishing@sbcglobal.net

Howard Publishing Press LLC is a Christian publishing company, ordained to publish the gift that God has given to those who are called to proclaim their message through writing.   It's our purpose to motivate and assist in spreading the Gospel of Jesus Christ by aiding God's people in fulfilling their God given purpose.   As a destiny helper, our purpose is also to help authors publish their material at an efficient low cost. We are a self-publishing company, publishing books for those who don't have the time or opportunity to do the legwork that's needed to produce quality work at an affordable cost.

Pastor R. Covington Sr.

www.ingramcontent.com/pod-product-compliance
Lightning Source LLC
Chambersburg PA
CBHW062005040426
42447CB00010B/1927